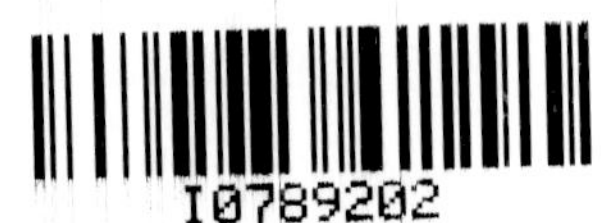
I0789202

RELAXING
COLORING BOOK

This book belongs to:

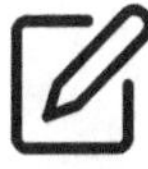 _______________________________________

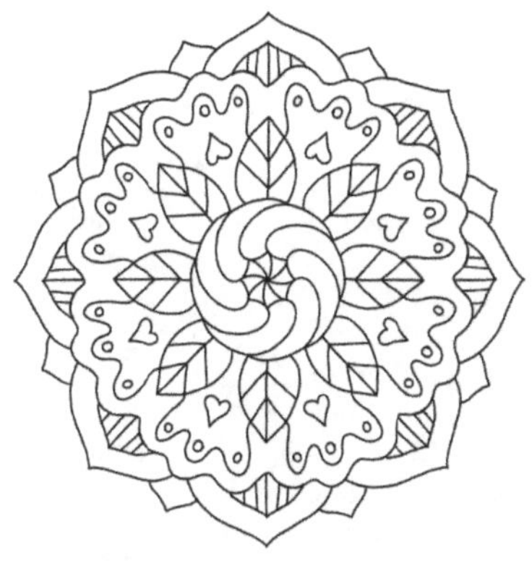

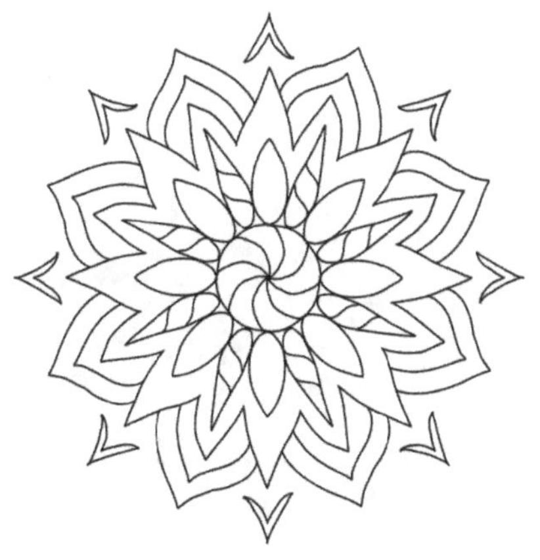

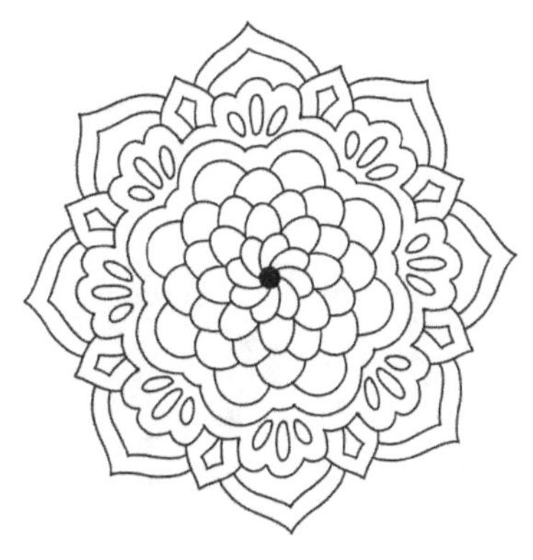

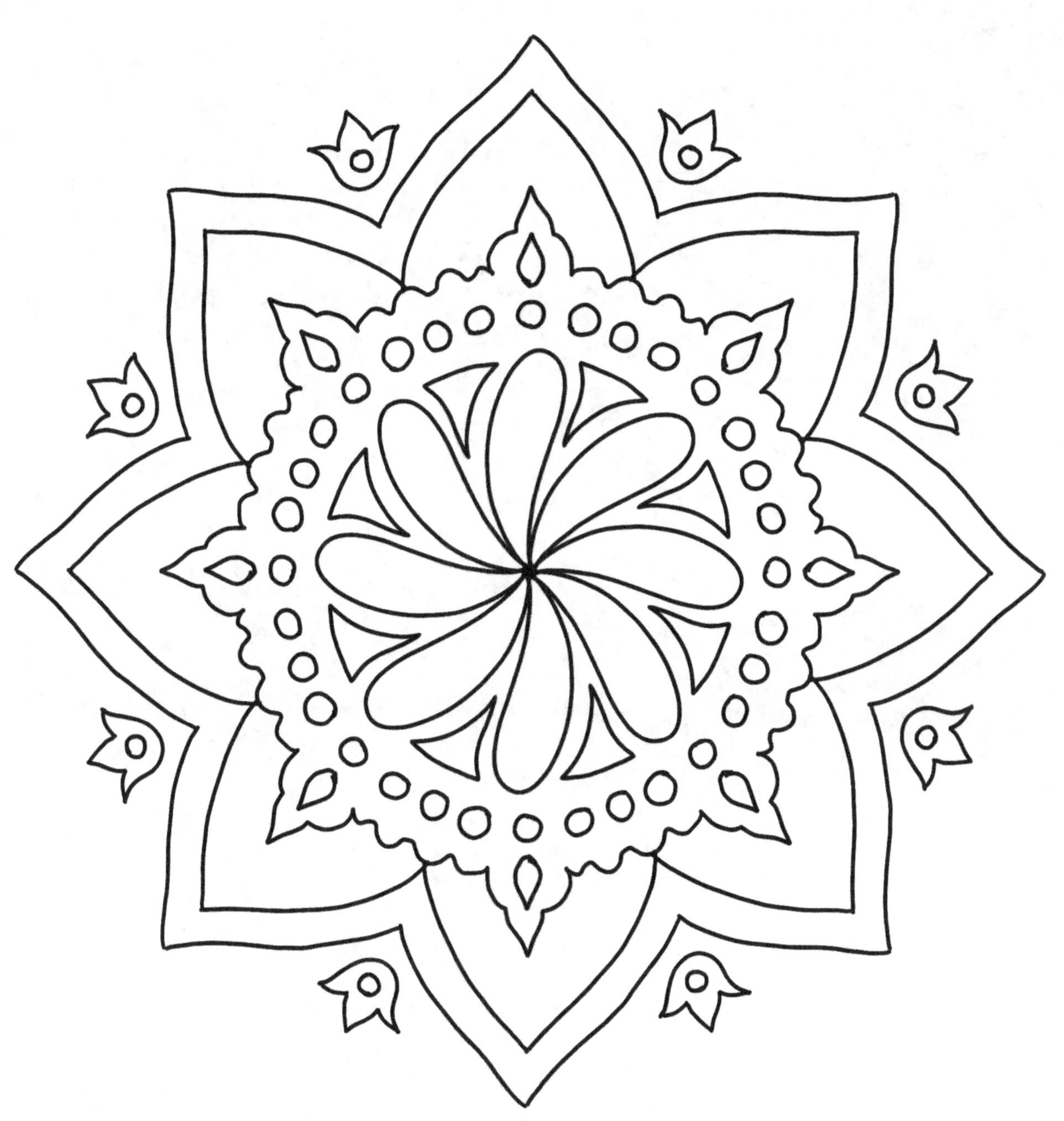

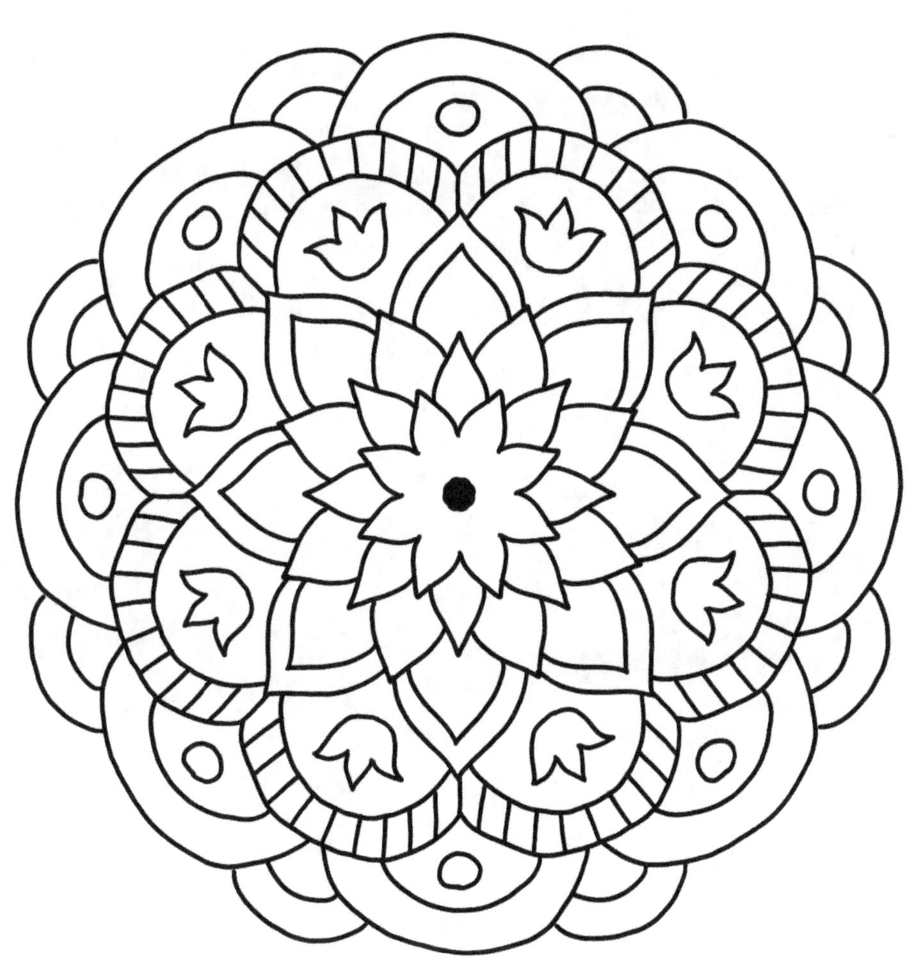

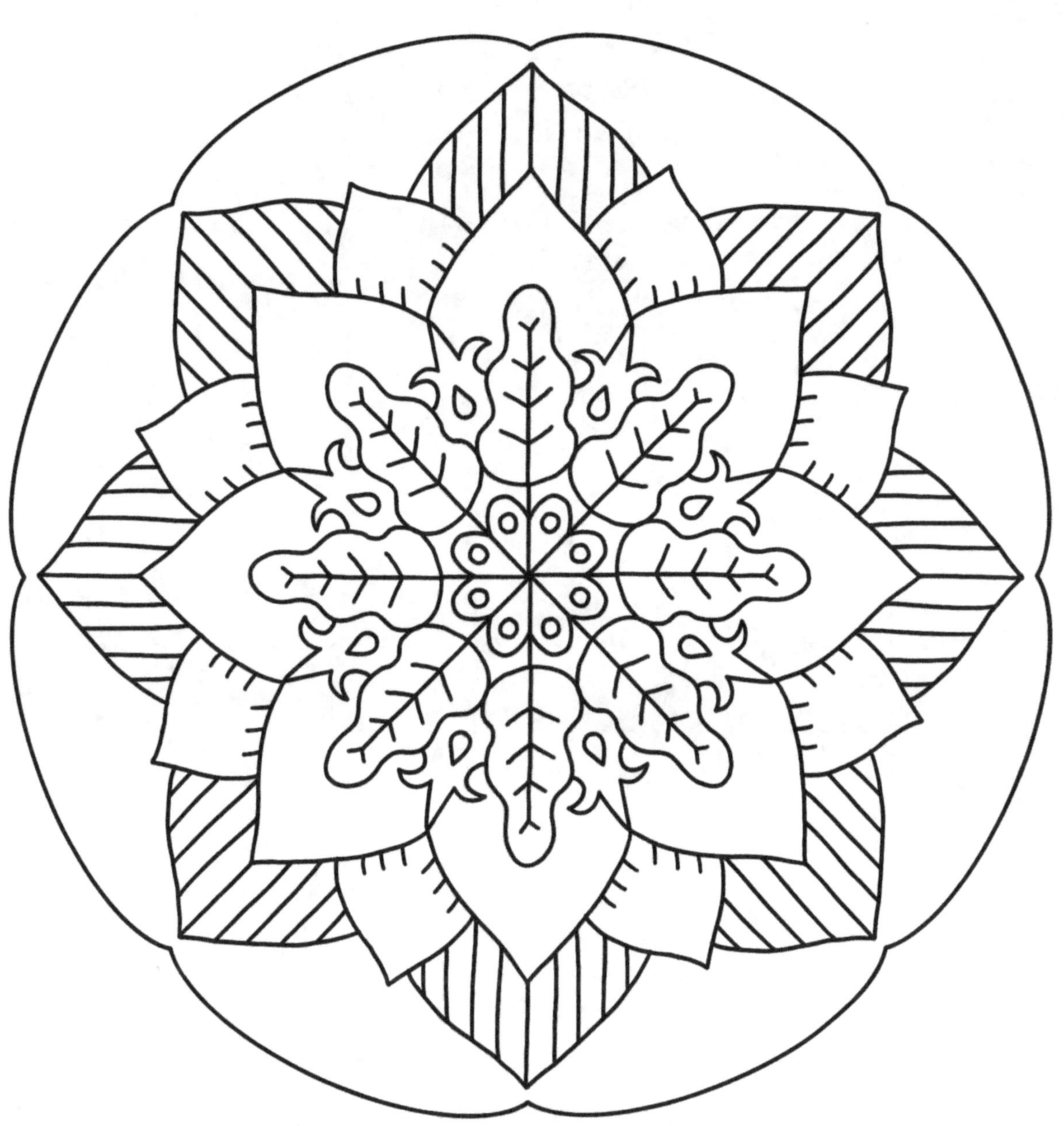

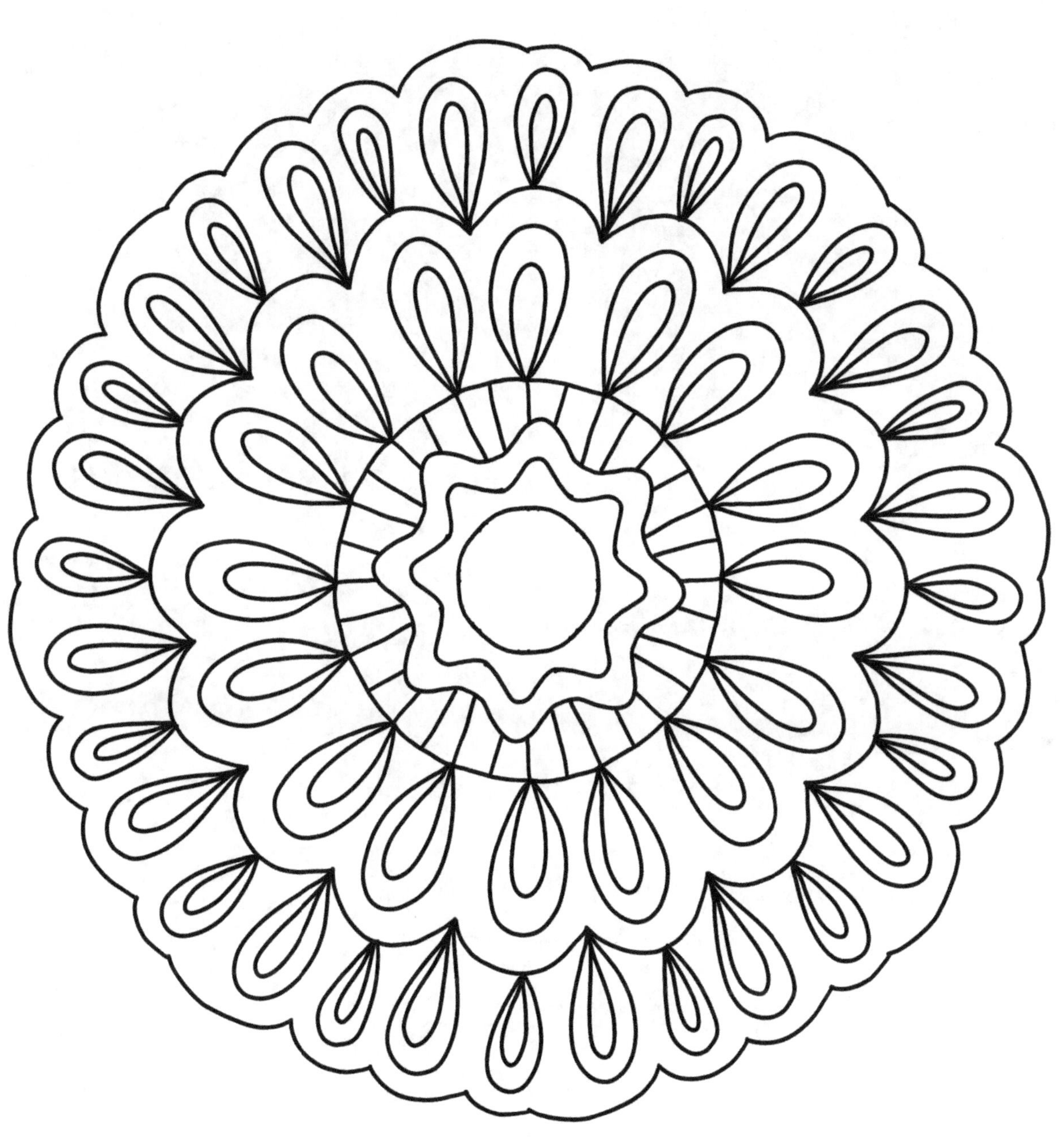

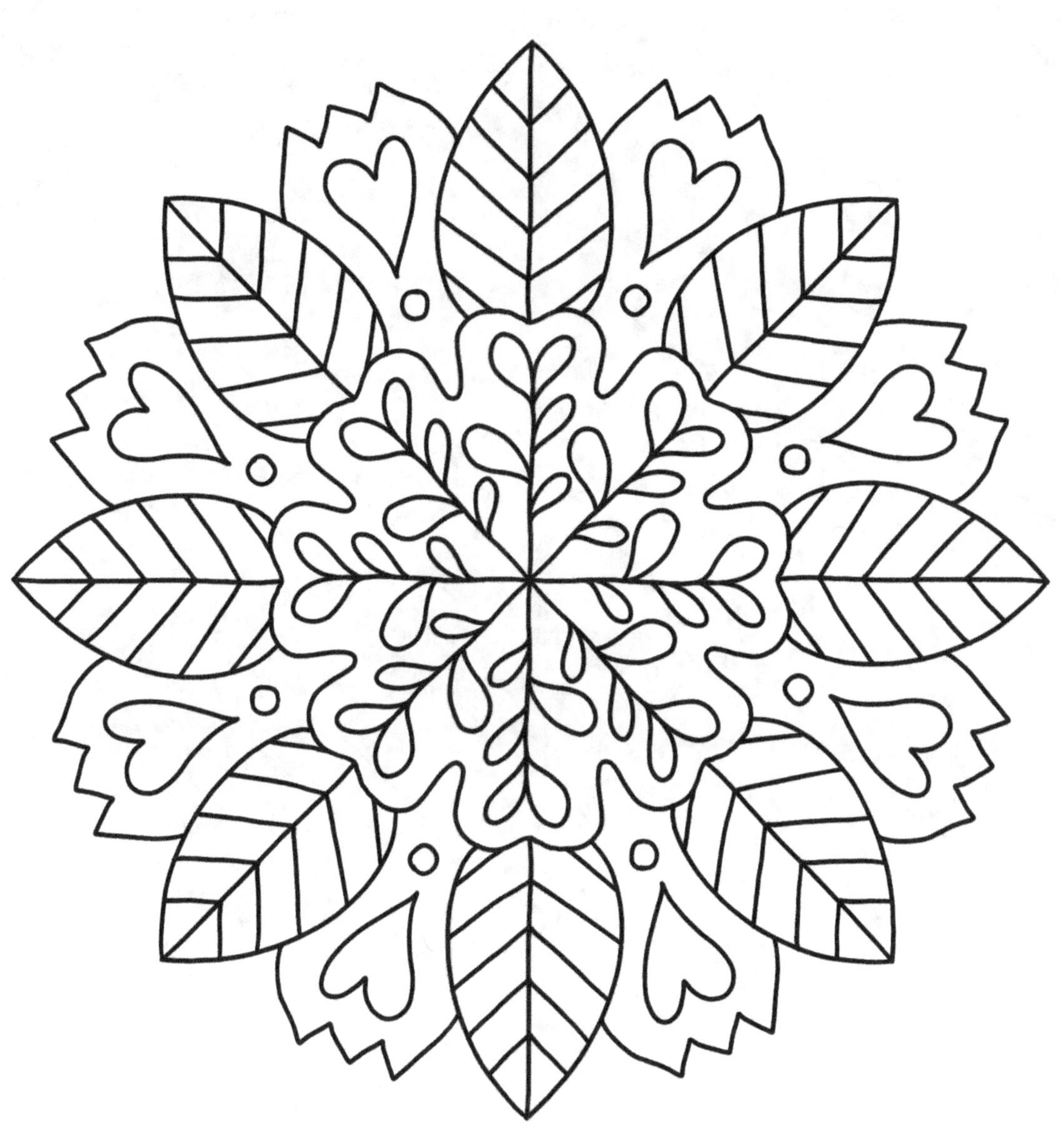

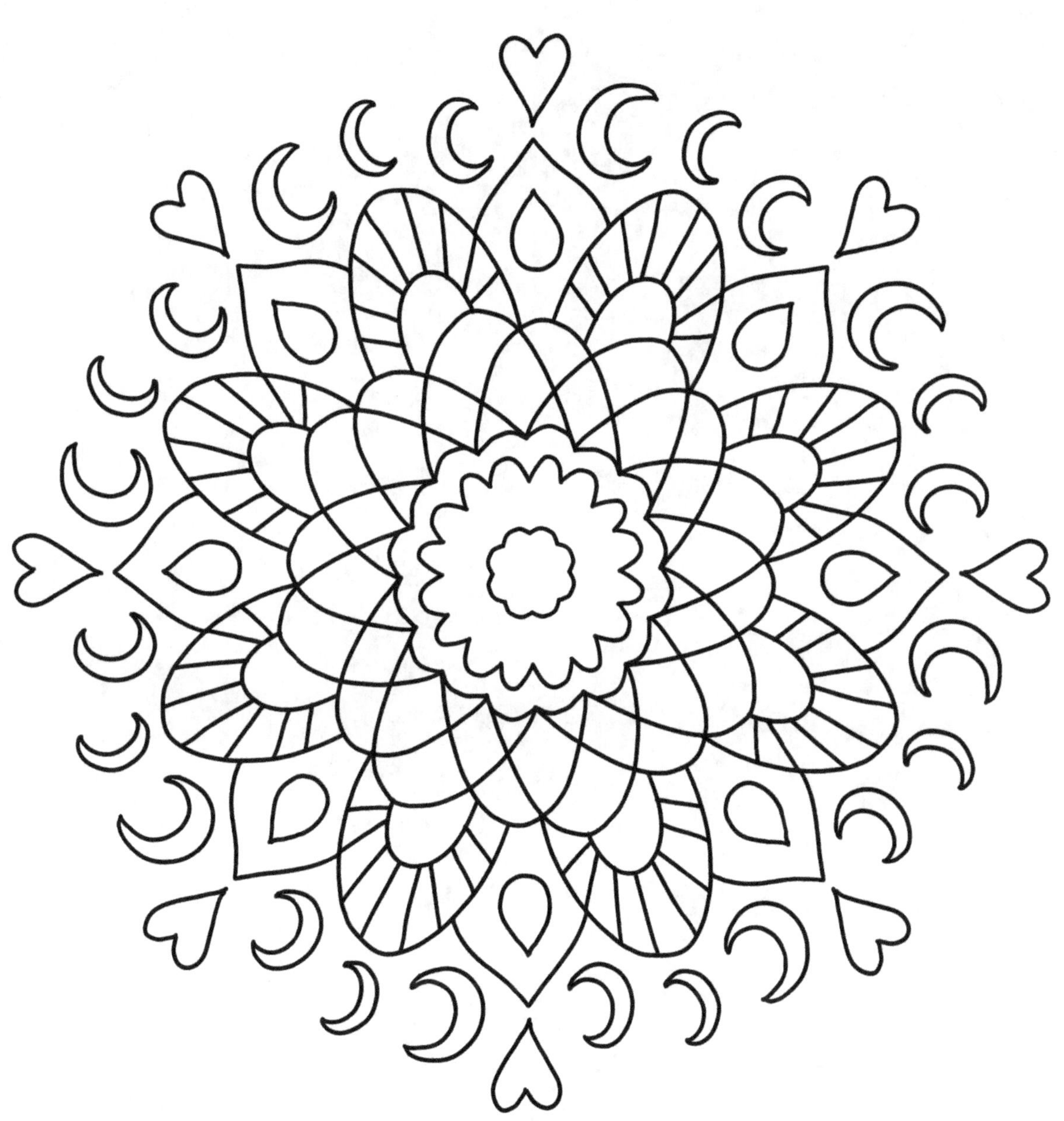

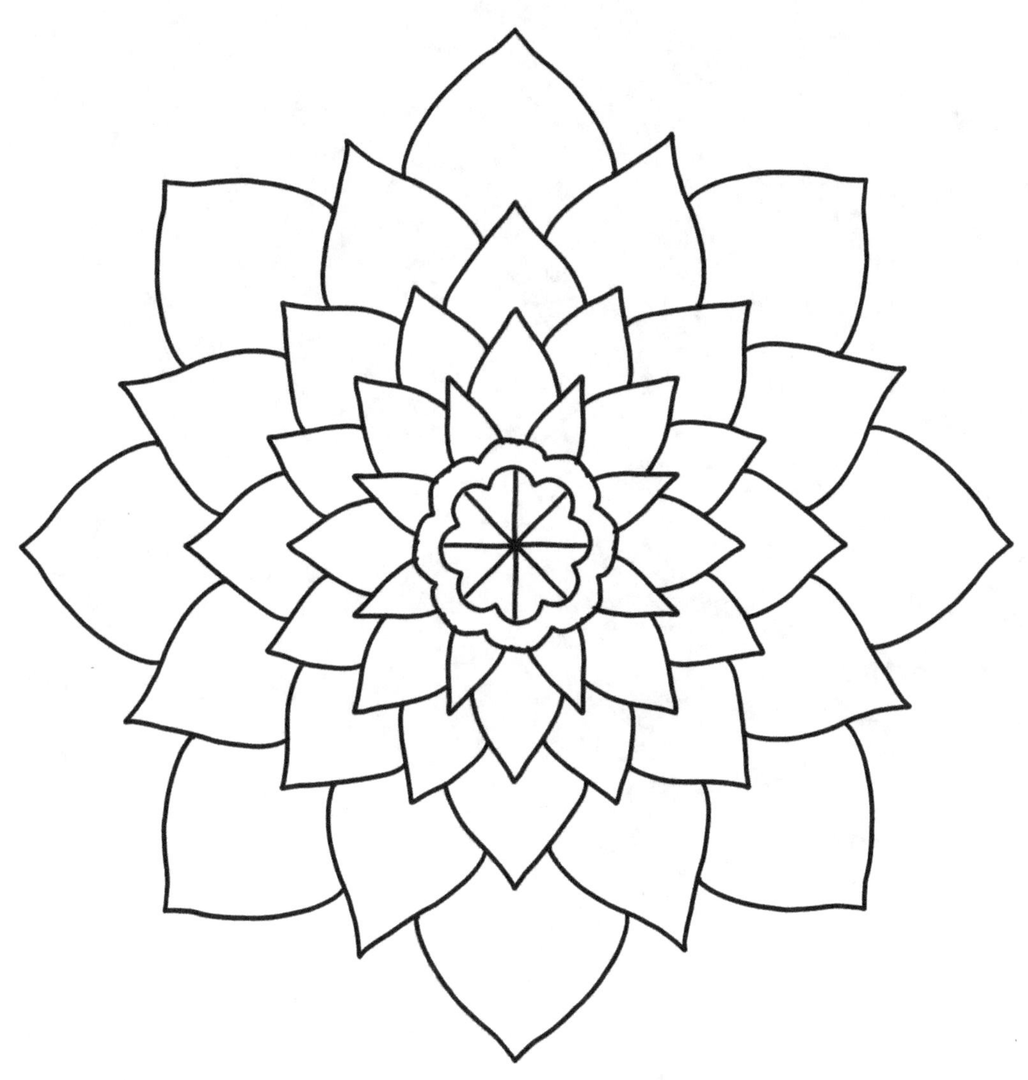

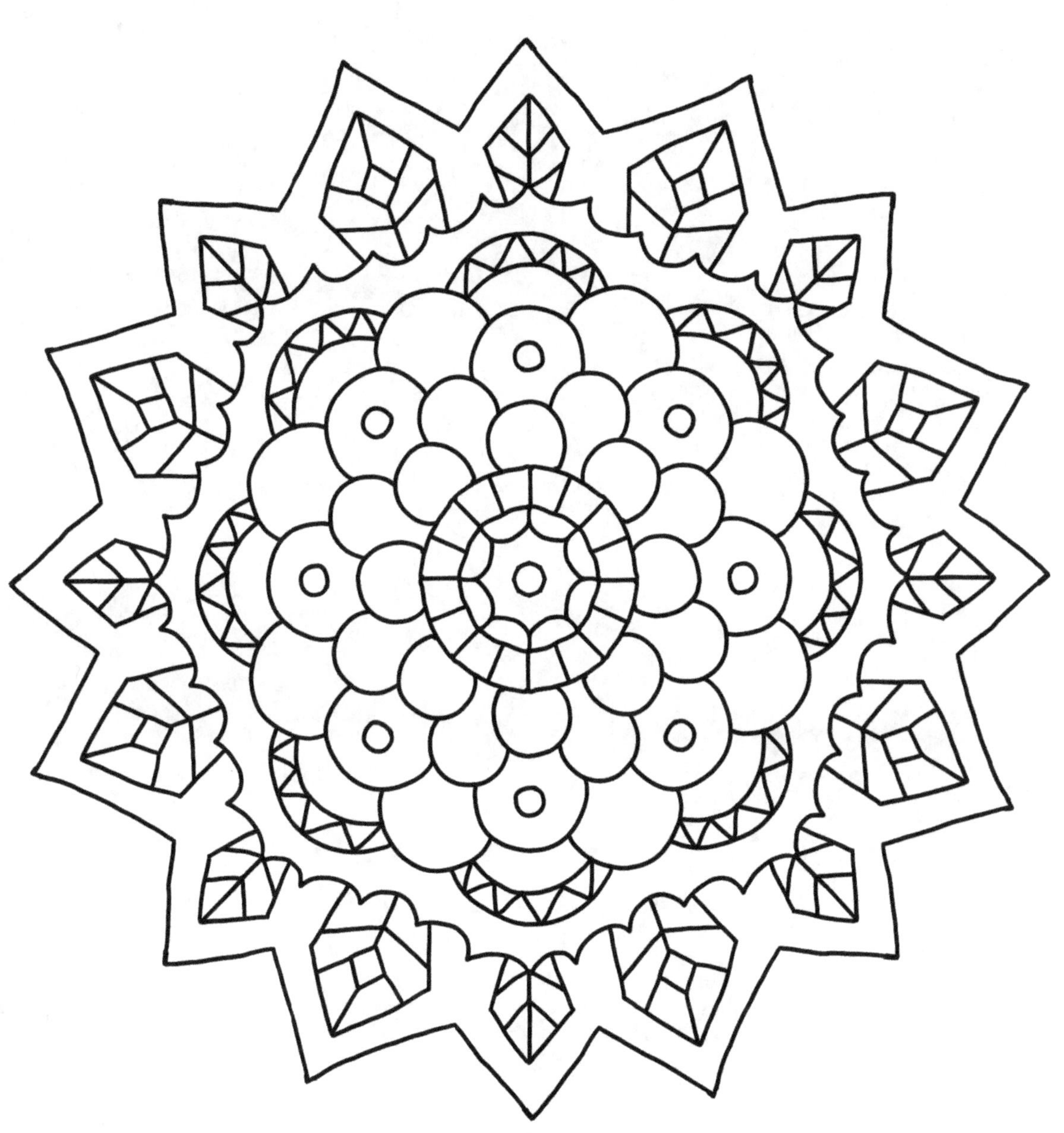

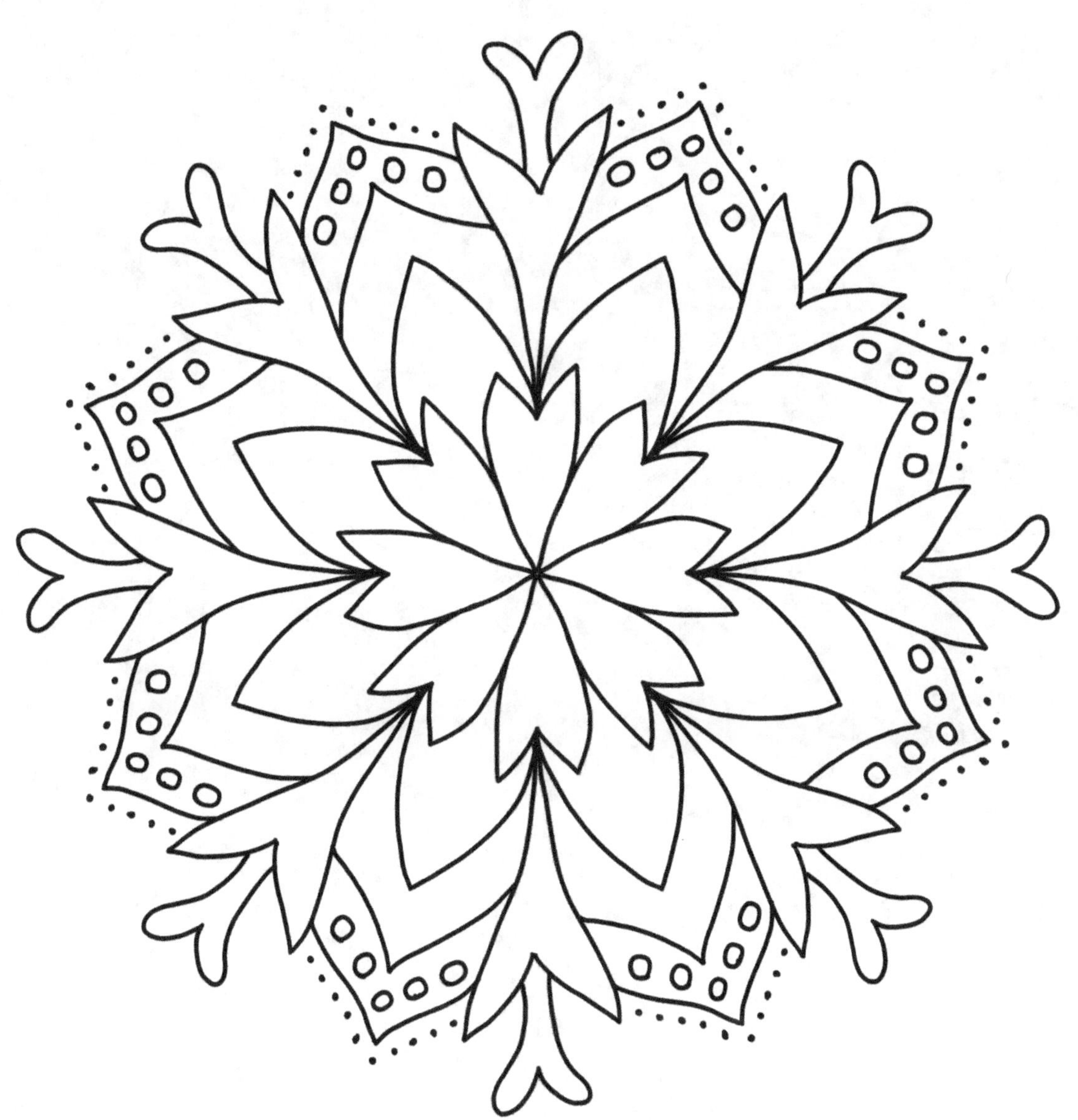

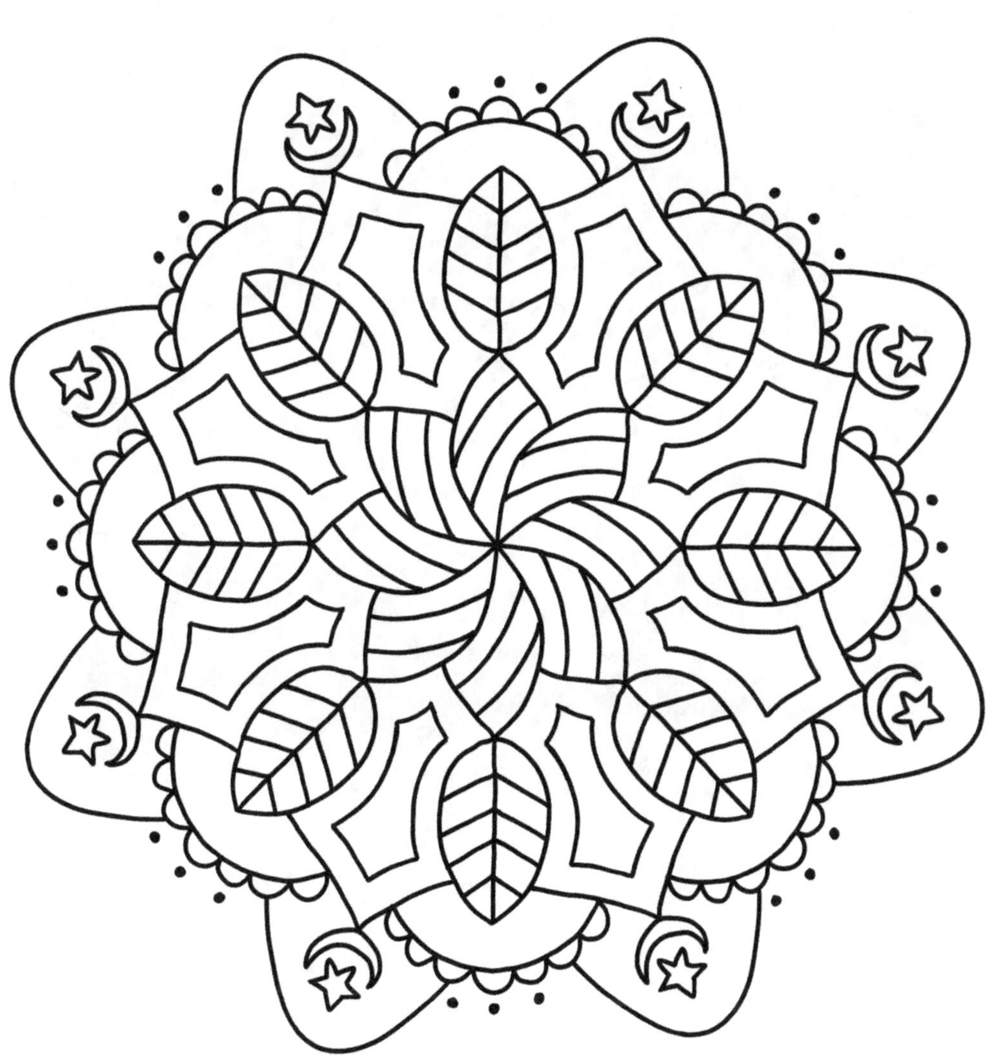

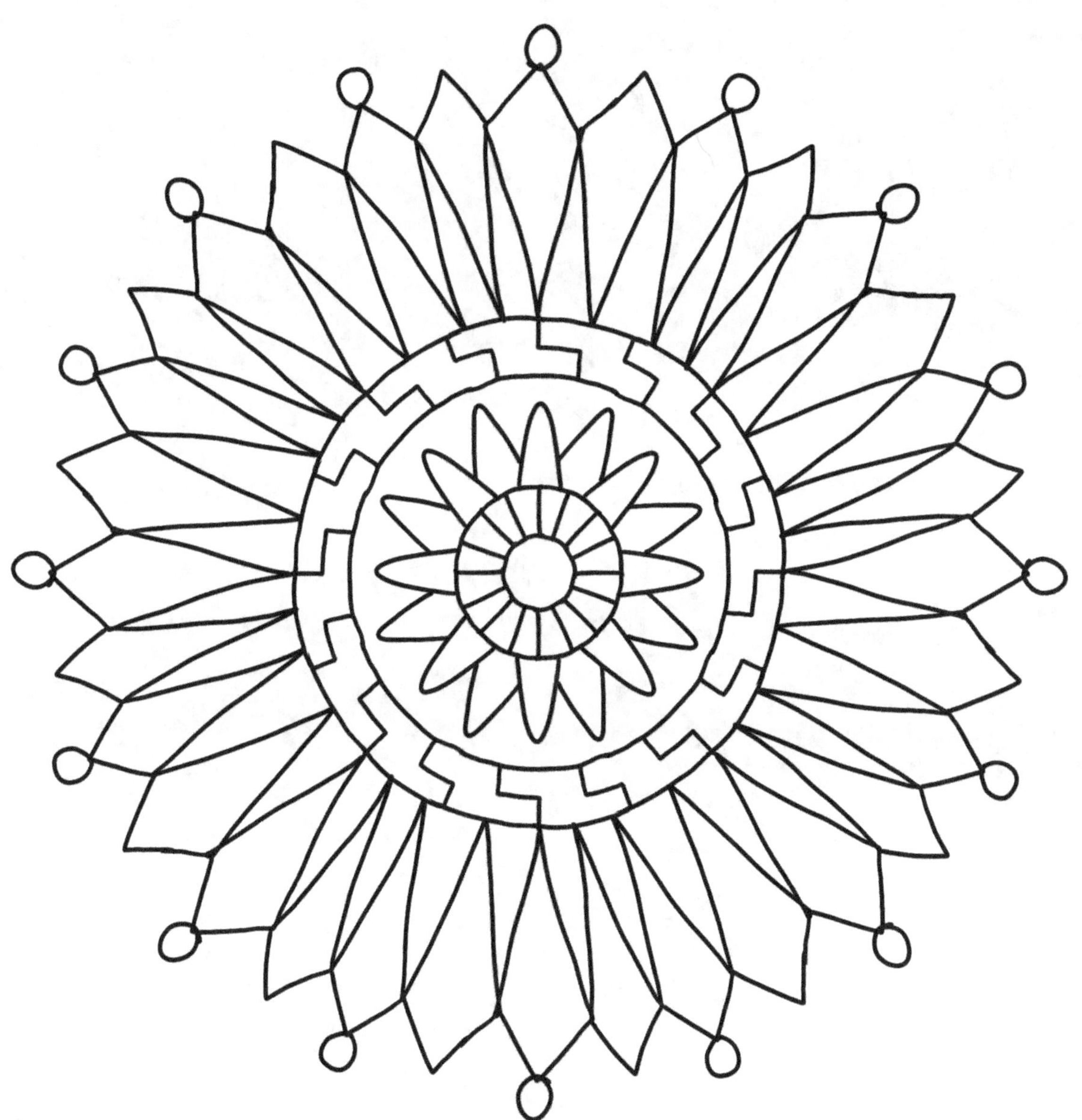

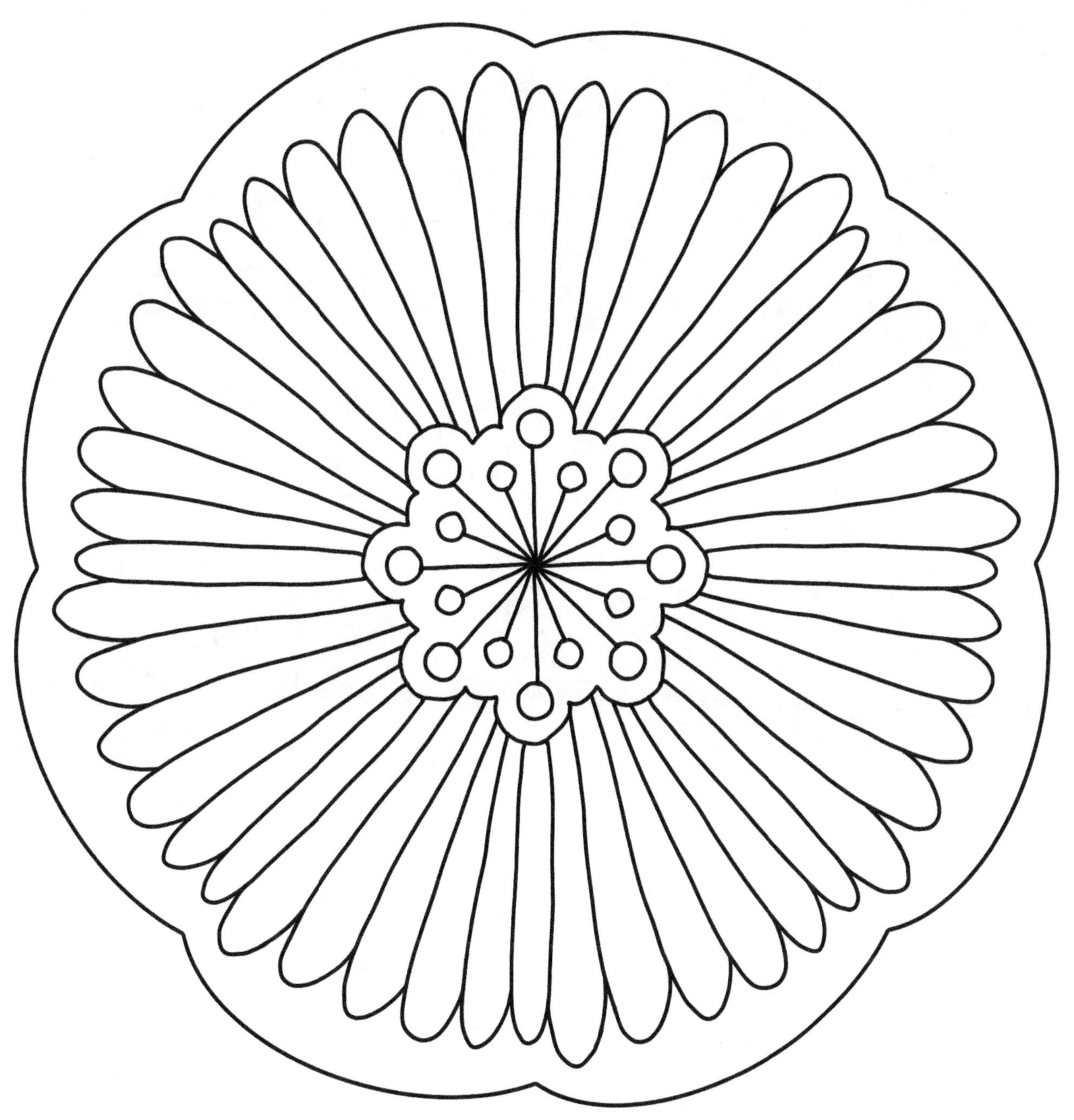

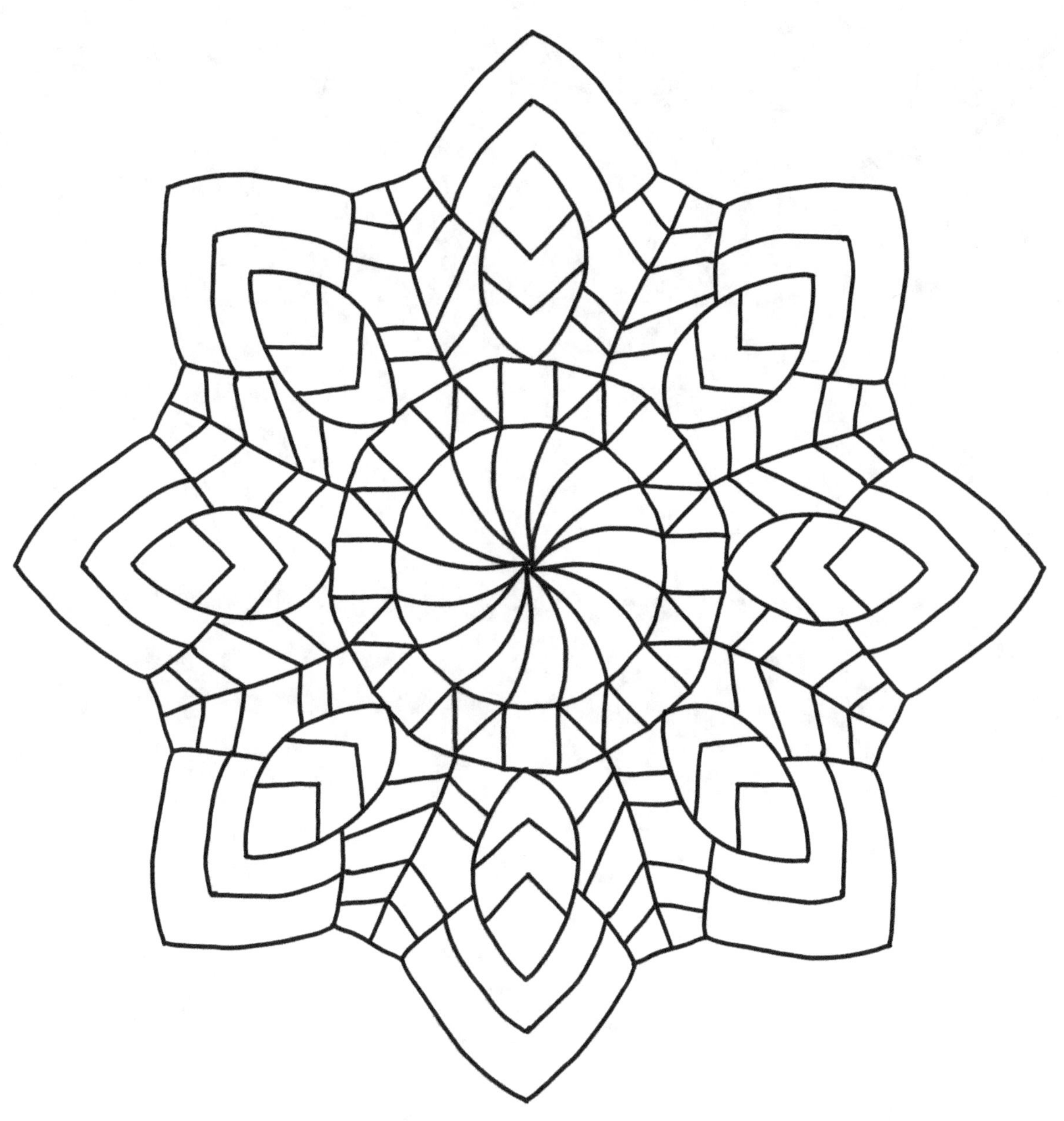

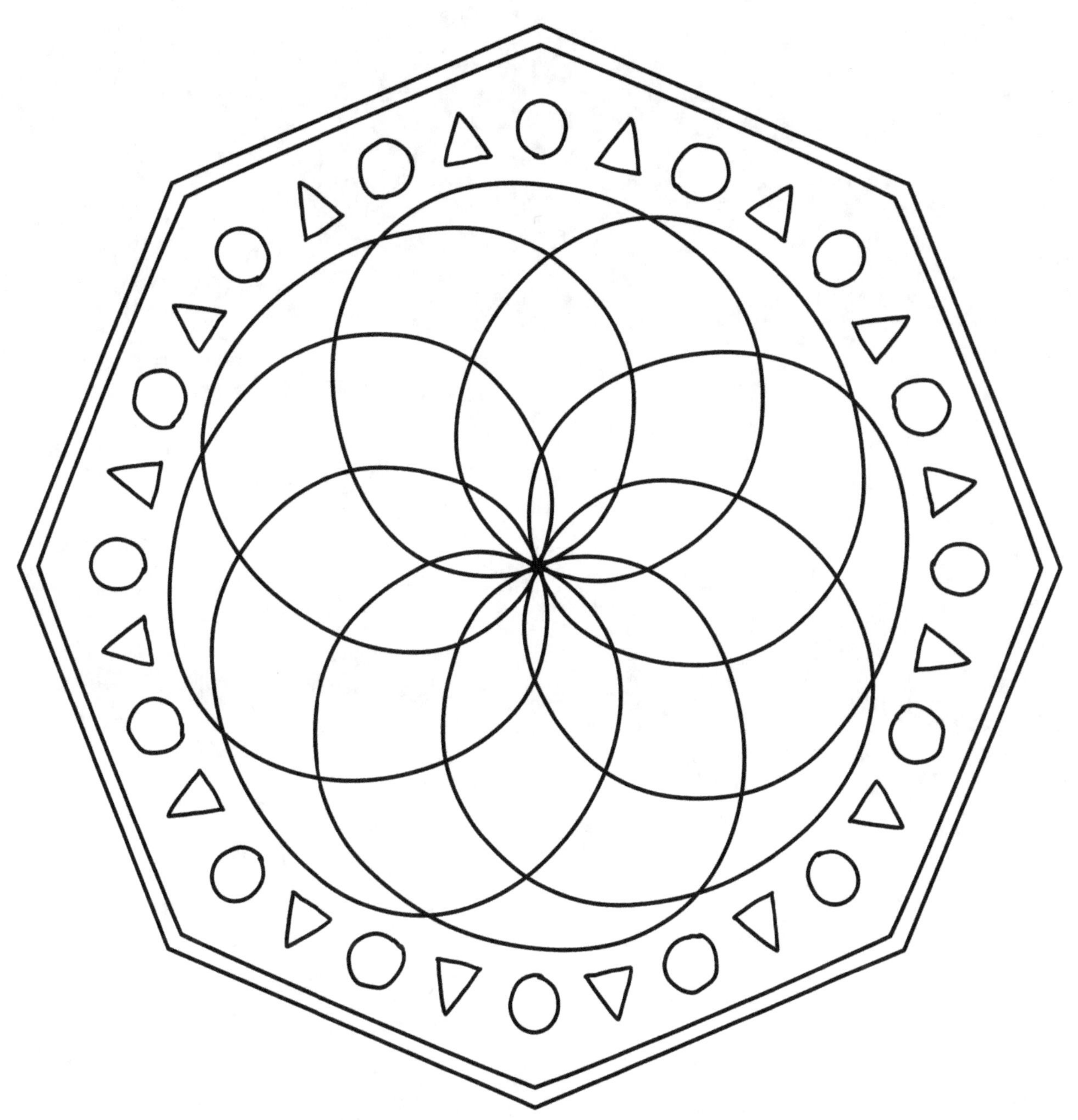

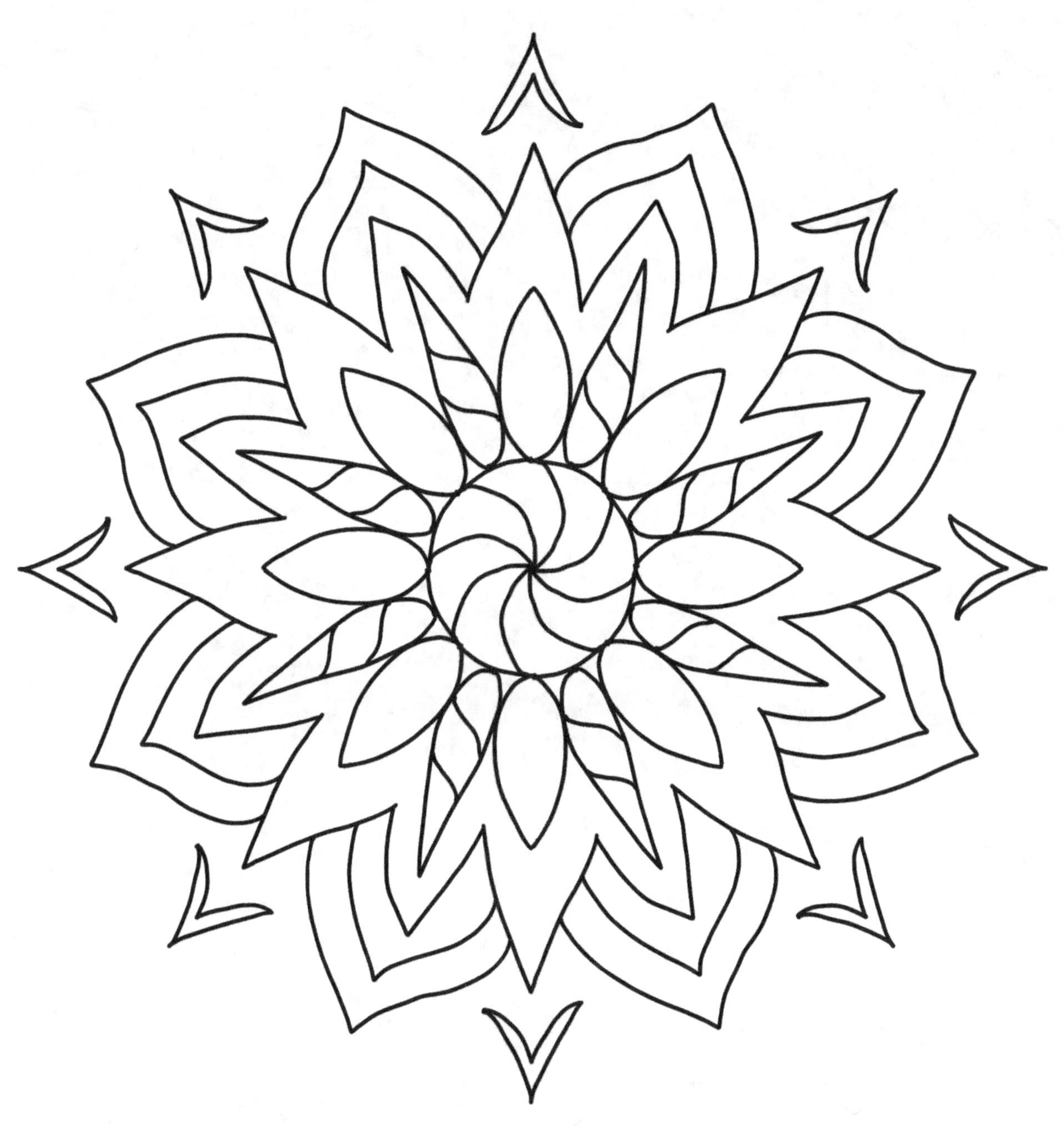

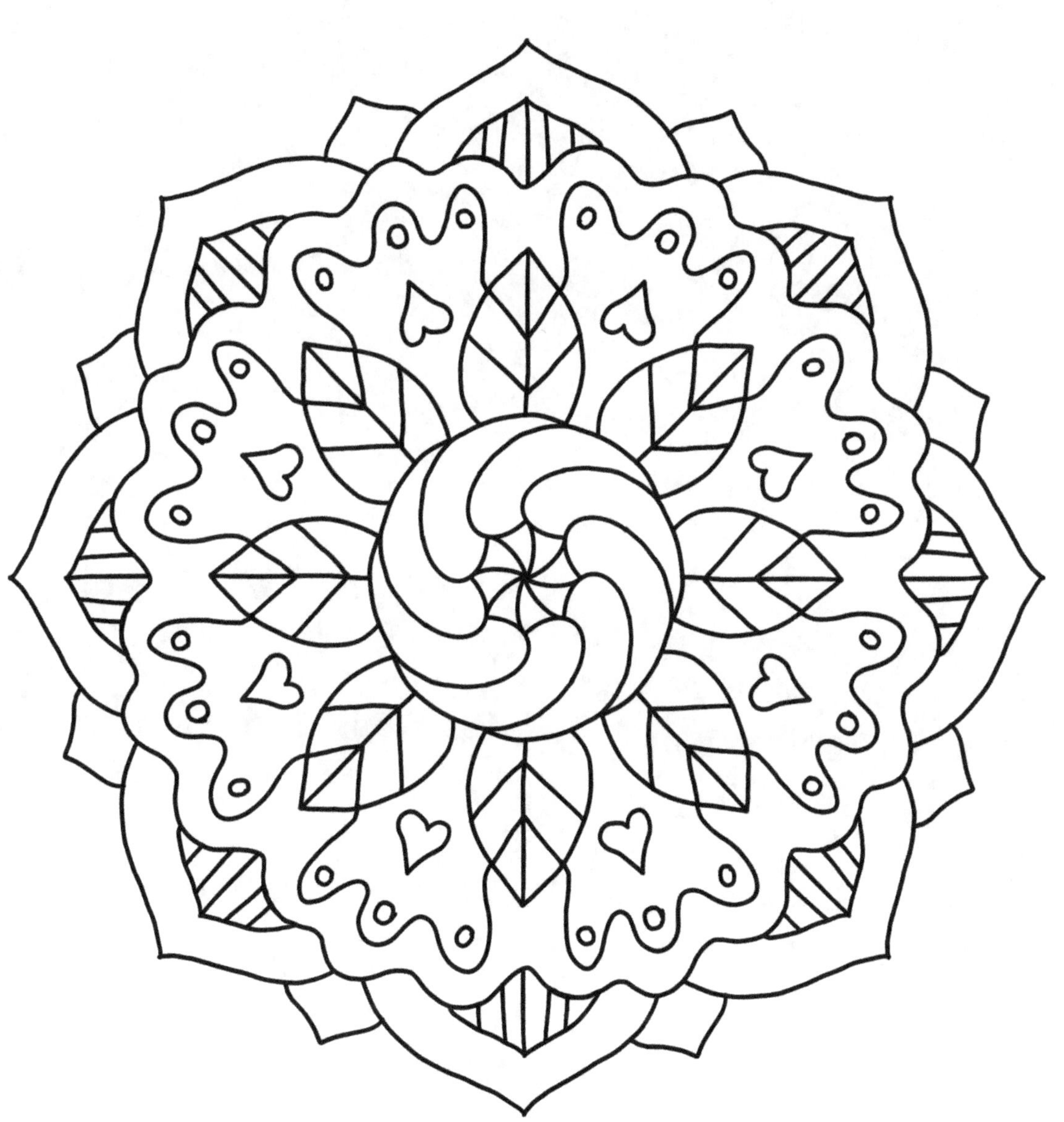

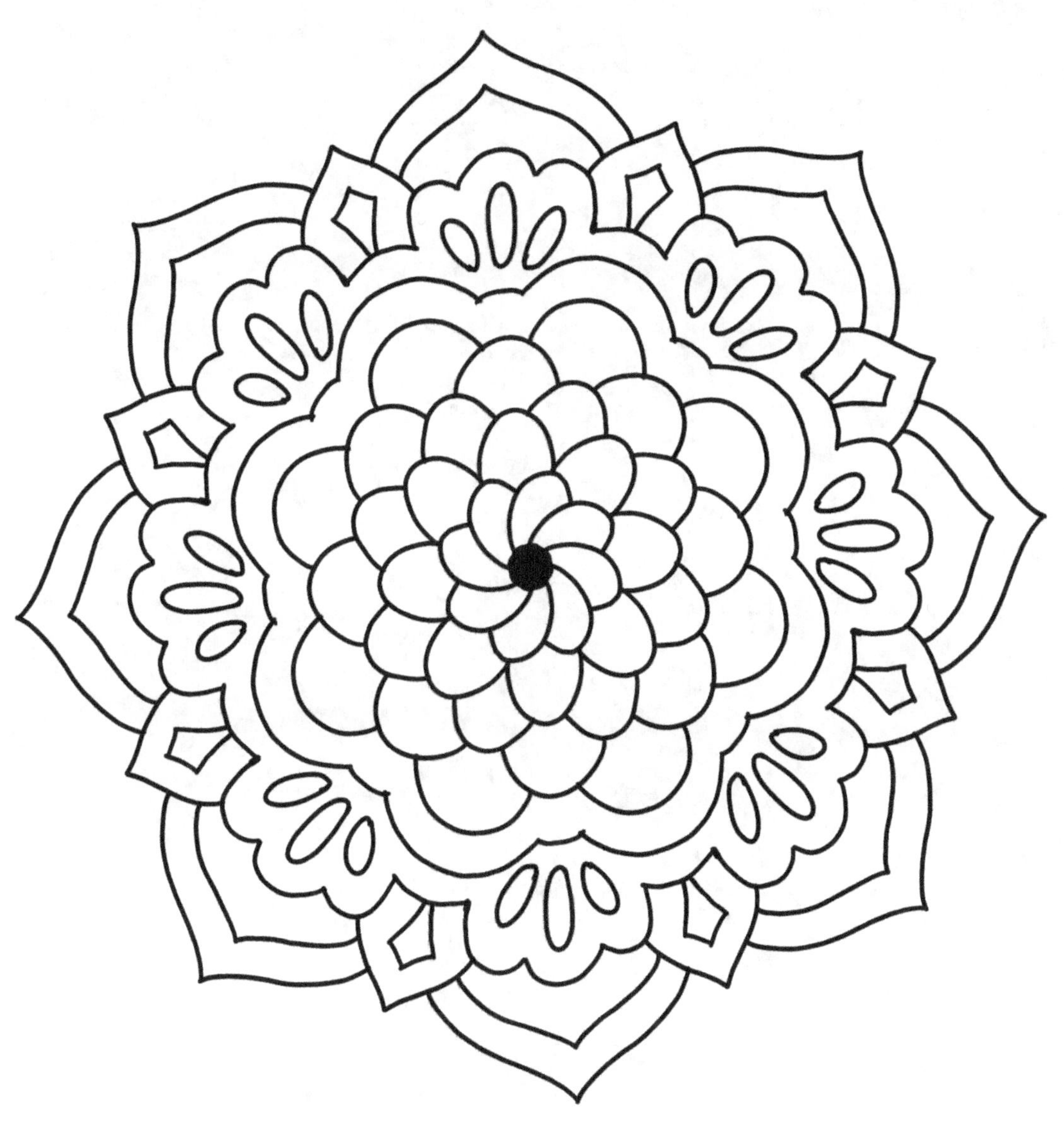

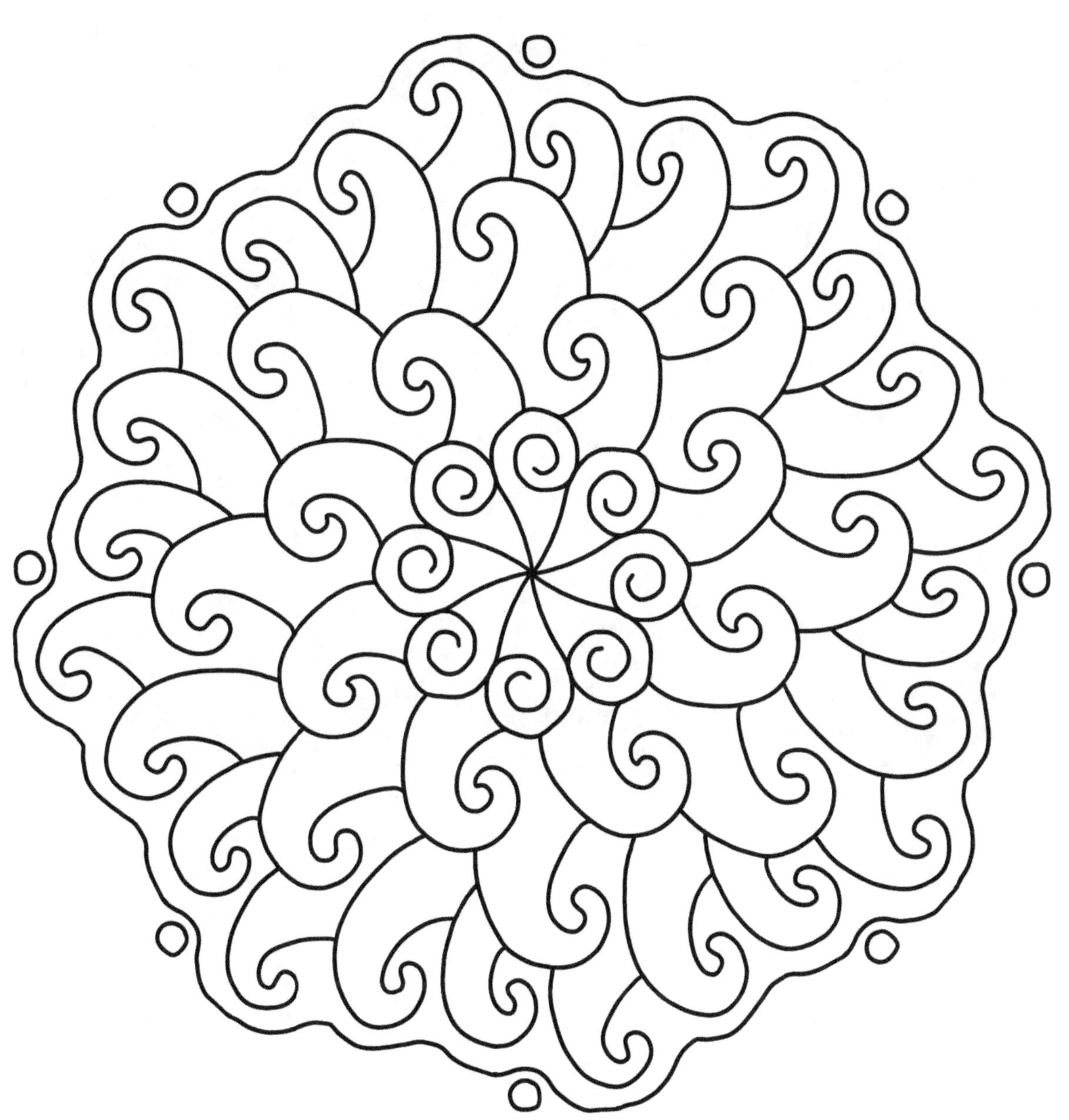

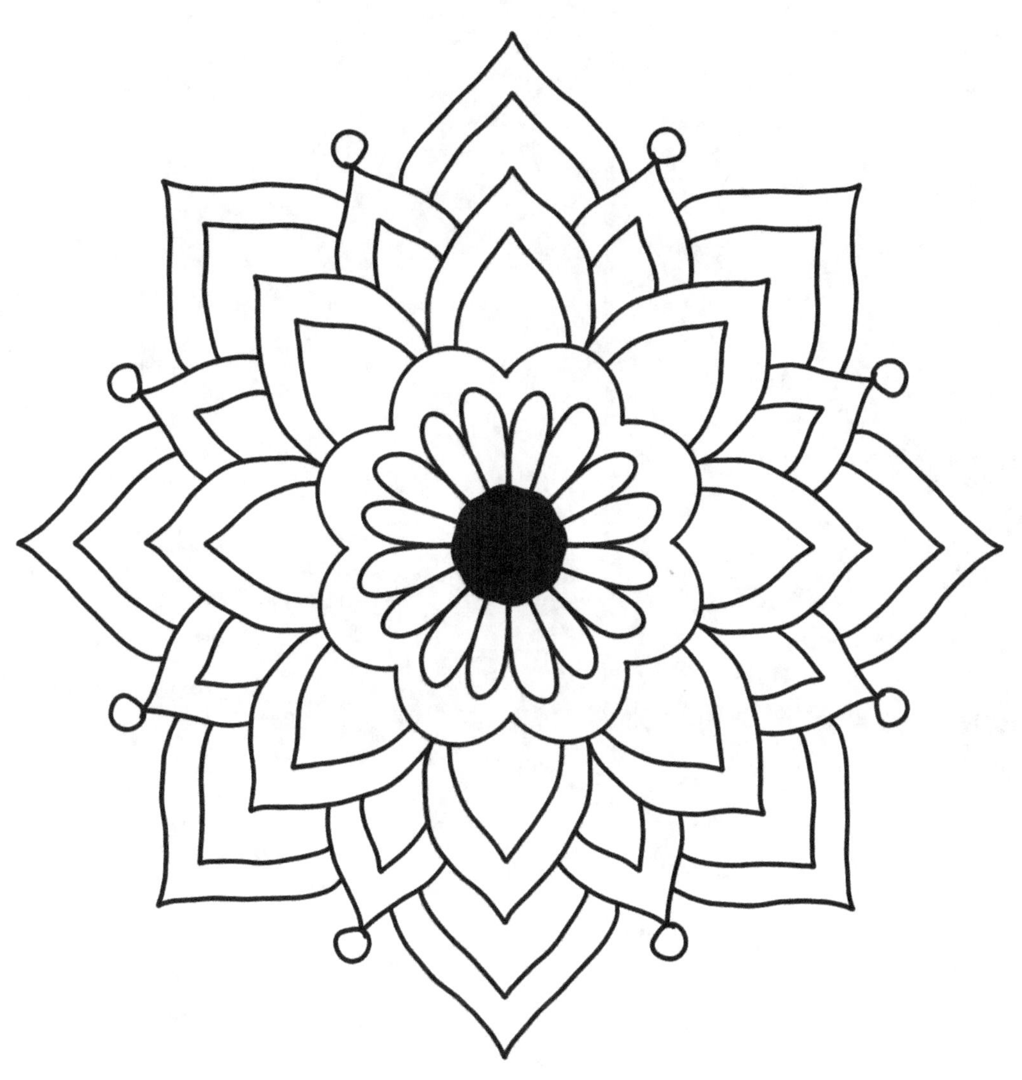

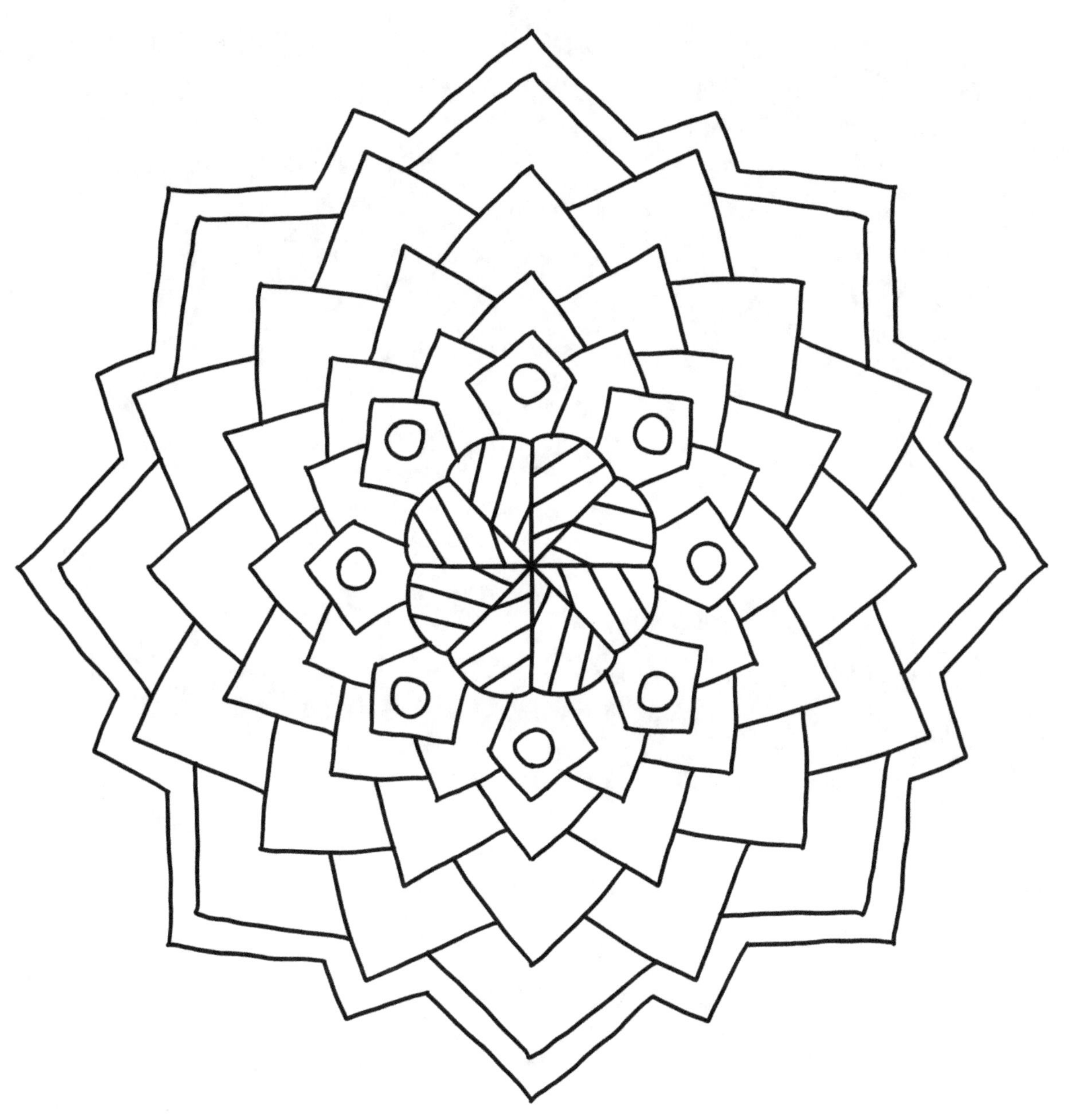

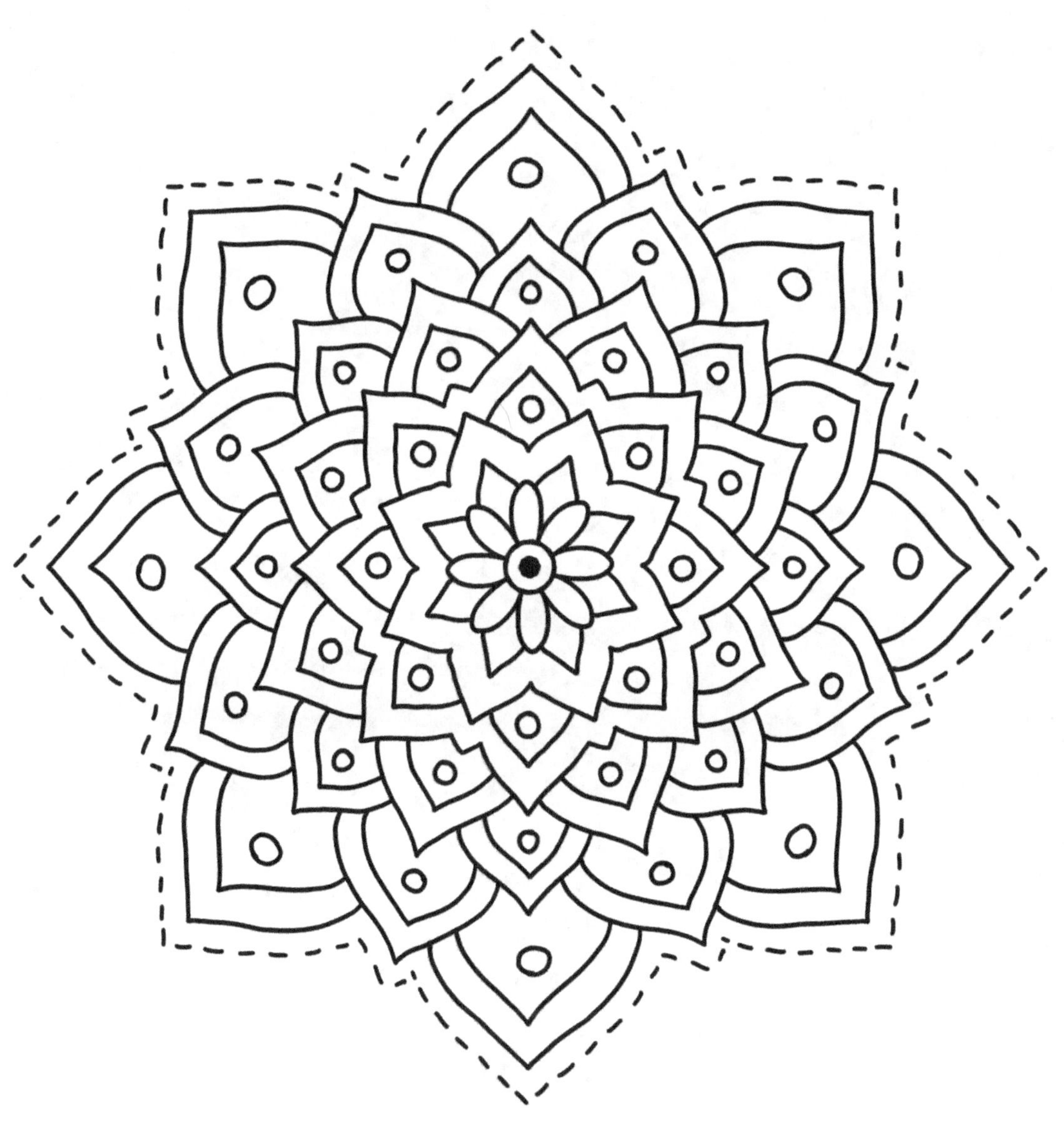

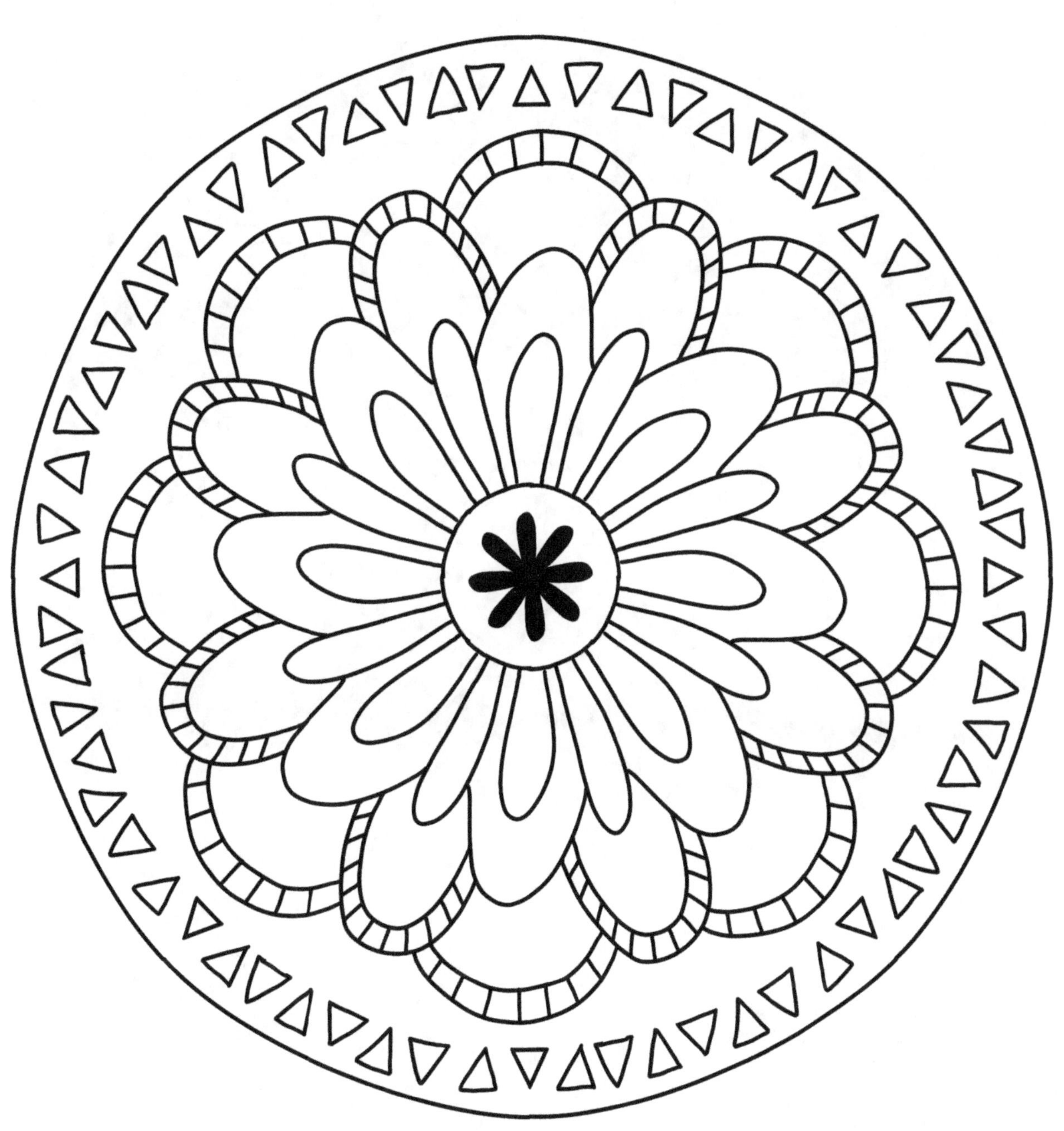

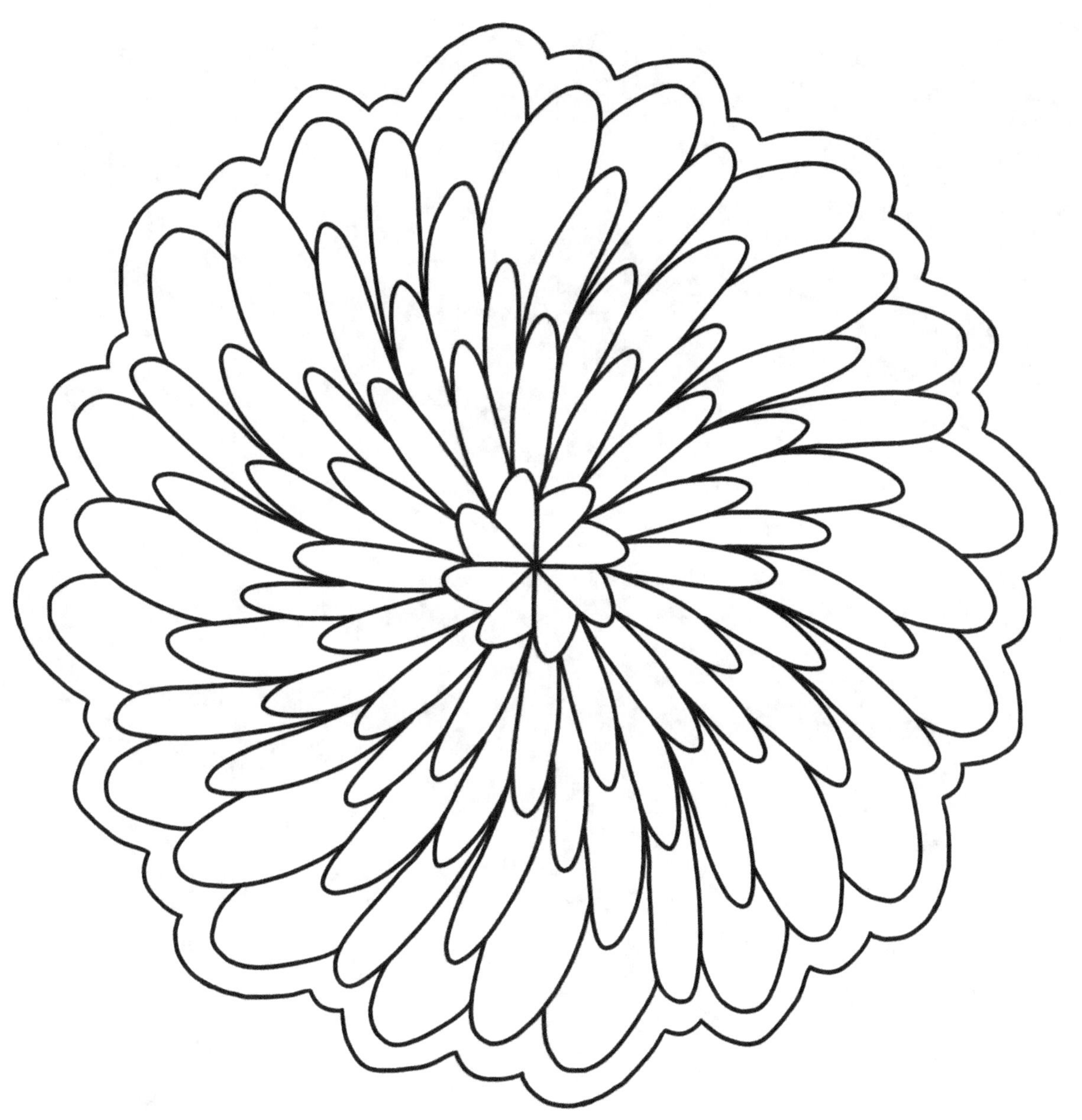

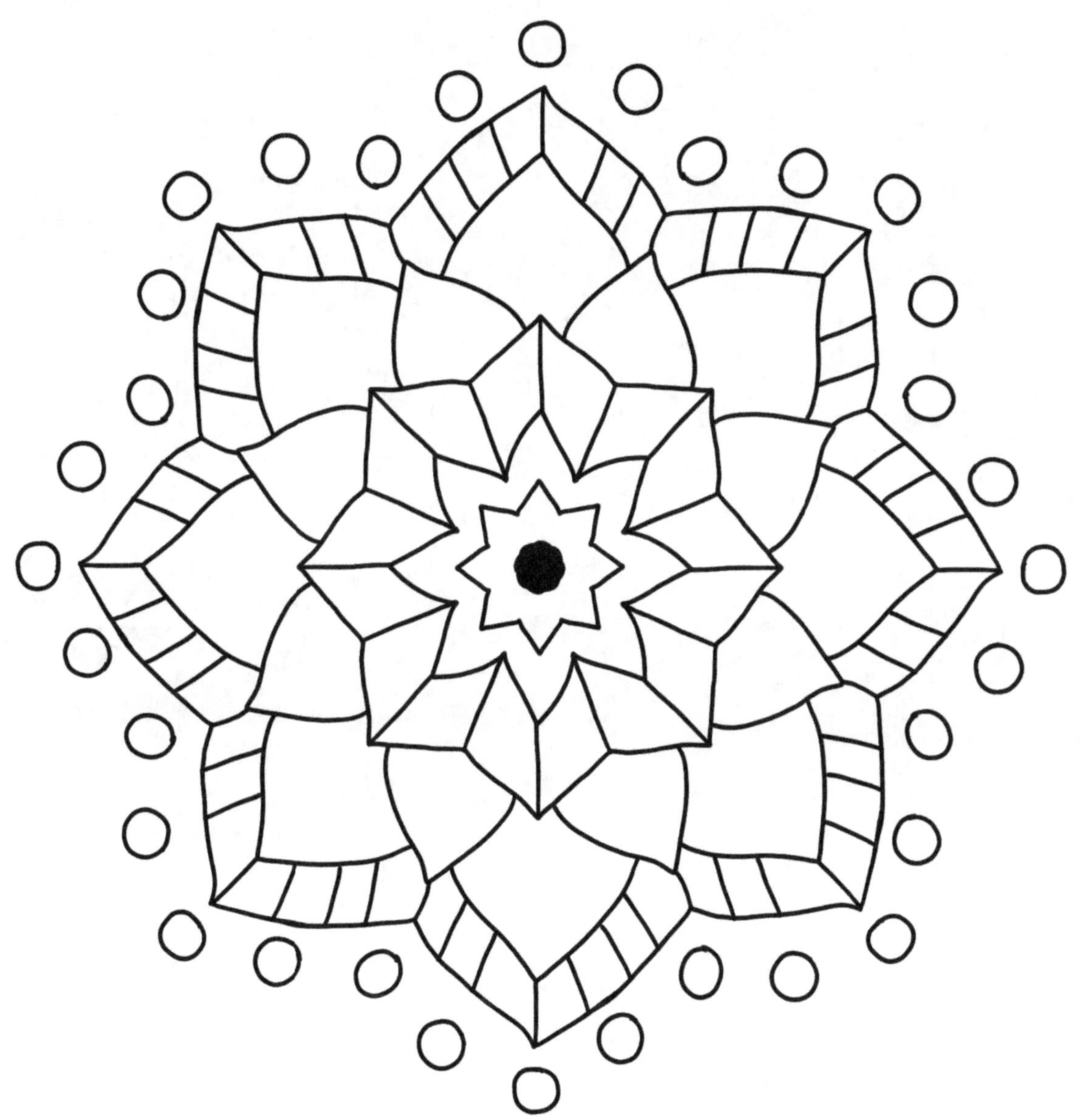

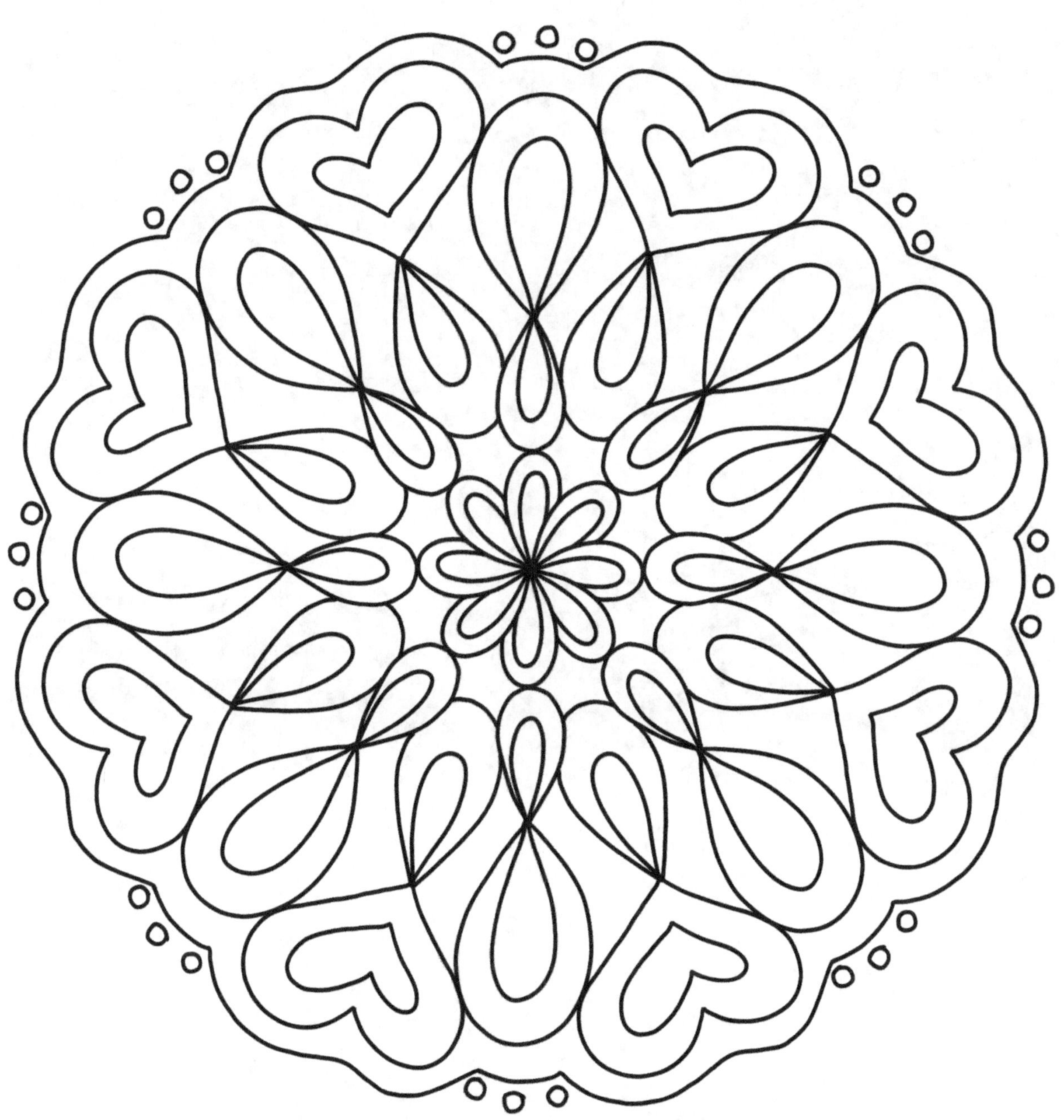

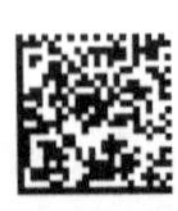

www.ingramcontent.com/pod-product-compliance
Lightning Source LLC
Chambersburg PA
CBHW081431250726
48654CB00013B/1907